CAR MAINTENANCE

LOGBOOK

THIS BELONGS TO

MAKE	MODEL
PHONE	EMAIL

CONTENTS PAGE

NAME	JOB / ROLE	EMAIL	PHONE

CAR INFORMATION

CAR MAKE	MODEL

YEAR	NEW / 2ND HAND	REGISTRATION NUMBER

SERIAL / VIN / CHASSIS NUMBER	OTHER

COLOR	BODY TYPE

MODIFICATION / DEFECT NOTES (ON PURCHASE)

OTHER NOTES

PURCHASE INFORMATION

PURCHASED FROM

DATE PURCHASED	PURCHASE PRICE	PICKED UP FROM

PHONE NUMBER	EMAIL

WARRANTY INFORMATION / NOTES

OTHER NOTES

INSURANCE INFORMATION

POLICY NUMBER	COMPANY	POLICY TYPE

START DATE	END DATE	NOTES

INSURANCE INFORMATION

POLICY NUMBER	COMPANY	POLICY TYPE

START DATE	END DATE	NOTES

OIL / OIL CHANGE

OIL FILTER PART NUMBER	SIZE OF PLUG
OIL NEEDED	AMOUNT NEEDED TO TOP UP

TIRE

LUG NUT SIZE	SIZE
NOTES	

AIR FILTER

PART NUMBER	MILEAGE BETWEEN CHANGES
NOTES	

FUEL FILTER

PART NUMBER	SUGGESTED MILEAGE BETWEEN CHANGES
NOTES	

FAN BELT

SIZE	SUGGESTED TIME BETWEEN CHANGES
NOTES	

SPARK PLUGS

SIZE	SUGGESTED TIME BETWEEN CHANGES
NOTES	

OIL CHANGE LOG

MILEAGE	OIL USED	MILES SINCE LAST CHANGE	DATE

MILEAGE	OIL USED	MILES SINCE LAST CHANGE	DATE

OIL CHANGE LOG

MILEAGE	OIL USED	MILES SINCE LAST CHANGE	DATE

MILEAGE	OIL USED	MILES SINCE LAST CHANGE	DATE

OIL CHANGE LOG

MILEAGE	OIL USED	MILES SINCE LAST CHANGE	DATE

MILEAGE	OIL USED	MILES SINCE LAST CHANGE	DATE

OIL CHANGE LOG

MILEAGE	OIL USED	MILES SINCE LAST CHANGE	DATE

MILEAGE	OIL USED	MILES SINCE LAST CHANGE	DATE

TIRE CHANGE LOG

MILEAGE	TIRES USED	TIRE(S) CHANGED	DATE

MILEAGE	TIRES USED	TIRE(S) CHANGED	DATE

TIRE CHANGE LOG

MILEAGE	TIRES USED	TIRE(S) CHANGED	DATE

MILEAGE	TIRES USED	TIRE(S) CHANGED	DATE

TIRE CHANGE LOG

MILEAGE	TIRES USED	TIRE(S) CHANGED	DATE

MILEAGE	TIRES USED	TIRE(S) CHANGED	DATE

AIR FILTER CHANGE LOG

MILEAGE	TIME SINCE LAST CHANGE	NOTES	DATE

MILEAGE	TIME SINCE LAST CHANGE	NOTES	DATE

FUEL FILTER CHANGE LOG

MILEAGE	TIME SINCE LAST CHANGE	NOTES	DATE

MILEAGE	TIME SINCE LAST CHANGE	NOTES	DATE

FAN BELT CHANGE LOG

MILEAGE	TIME SINCE LAST CHANGE	NOTES	DATE

MILEAGE	TIME SINCE LAST CHANGE	NOTES	DATE

SPARK PLUG CHANGE LOG

MILEAGE	TIME SINCE LAST CHANGE	NOTES	DATE

MILEAGE	TIME SINCE LAST CHANGE	NOTES	DATE

SERVICE / REPAIR / MODIFICATIONS

MILEAGE	DESCRIPTION / INFORMATION

WORK DONE BY	NOTES / WARRANTY	DATE / TIME

SERVICE / REPAIR / MODIFICATIONS

MILEAGE	DESCRIPTION / INFORMATION

WORK DONE BY	NOTES / WARRANTY	DATE / TIME

SERVICE / REPAIR / MODIFICATIONS

MILEAGE	DESCRIPTION / INFORMATION

WORK DONE BY	NOTES / WARRANTY	DATE / TIME

SERVICE / REPAIR / MODIFICATIONS

MILEAGE	DESCRIPTION / INFORMATION

WORK DONE BY	NOTES / WARRANTY	DATE / TIME

SERVICE / REPAIR / MODIFICATIONS

MILEAGE	DESCRIPTION / INFORMATION

WORK DONE BY	NOTES / WARRANTY	DATE / TIME

SERVICE / REPAIR / MODIFICATIONS

MILEAGE	DESCRIPTION / INFORMATION

WORK DONE BY	NOTES / WARRANTY	DATE / TIME

SERVICE / REPAIR / MODIFICATIONS

MILEAGE	DESCRIPTION / INFORMATION

WORK DONE BY	NOTES / WARRANTY	DATE / TIME

MILEAGE	DESCRIPTION / INFORMATION

WORK DONE BY	NOTES / WARRANTY	DATE / TIME

SERVICE / REPAIR / MODIFICATIONS

MILEAGE	DESCRIPTION / INFORMATION

WORK DONE BY	NOTES / WARRANTY	DATE / TIME

SERVICE / REPAIR / MODIFICATIONS

MILEAGE	DESCRIPTION / INFORMATION

WORK DONE BY	NOTES / WARRANTY	DATE / TIME

SERVICE / REPAIR / MODIFICATIONS

MILEAGE	DESCRIPTION / INFORMATION

WORK DONE BY	NOTES / WARRANTY	DATE / TIME

SERVICE / REPAIR / MODIFICATIONS

MILEAGE	DESCRIPTION / INFORMATION

WORK DONE BY	NOTES / WARRANTY	DATE / TIME

MILEAGE	DESCRIPTION / INFORMATION

WORK DONE BY	NOTES / WARRANTY	DATE / TIME

MILEAGE	DESCRIPTION / INFORMATION

WORK DONE BY	NOTES / WARRANTY	DATE / TIME

SERVICE / REPAIR / MODIFICATIONS

MILEAGE	DESCRIPTION / INFORMATION

WORK DONE BY	NOTES / WARRANTY	DATE / TIME

MILEAGE	DESCRIPTION / INFORMATION

WORK DONE BY	NOTES / WARRANTY	DATE / TIME

MILEAGE	DESCRIPTION / INFORMATION

WORK DONE BY	NOTES / WARRANTY	DATE / TIME

SERVICE / REPAIR / MODIFICATIONS

MILEAGE	DESCRIPTION / INFORMATION

WORK DONE BY	NOTES / WARRANTY	DATE / TIME

SERVICE / REPAIR / MODIFICATIONS

MILEAGE	DESCRIPTION / INFORMATION

WORK DONE BY	NOTES / WARRANTY	DATE / TIME

MILEAGE	DESCRIPTION / INFORMATION

WORK DONE BY	NOTES / WARRANTY	DATE / TIME

MILEAGE	DESCRIPTION / INFORMATION

WORK DONE BY	NOTES / WARRANTY	DATE / TIME

SERVICE / REPAIR / MODIFICATIONS

MILEAGE	DESCRIPTION / INFORMATION

WORK DONE BY	NOTES / WARRANTY	DATE / TIME

SERVICE / REPAIR / MODIFICATIONS

MILEAGE	DESCRIPTION / INFORMATION

WORK DONE BY	NOTES / WARRANTY	DATE / TIME

SERVICE / REPAIR / MODIFICATIONS

MILEAGE	DESCRIPTION / INFORMATION

WORK DONE BY	NOTES / WARRANTY	DATE / TIME

SERVICE / REPAIR / MODIFICATIONS

MILEAGE	DESCRIPTION / INFORMATION

WORK DONE BY	NOTES / WARRANTY	DATE / TIME

SERVICE / REPAIR / MODIFICATIONS

MILEAGE	DESCRIPTION / INFORMATION

WORK DONE BY	NOTES / WARRANTY	DATE / TIME

SERVICE / REPAIR / MODIFICATIONS

MILEAGE	DESCRIPTION / INFORMATION

WORK DONE BY	NOTES / WARRANTY	DATE / TIME

MILEAGE	DESCRIPTION / INFORMATION

WORK DONE BY	NOTES / WARRANTY	DATE / TIME

SERVICE / REPAIR / MODIFICATIONS

MILEAGE	DESCRIPTION / INFORMATION

WORK DONE BY	NOTES / WARRANTY	DATE / TIME

MILEAGE	DESCRIPTION / INFORMATION

WORK DONE BY	NOTES / WARRANTY	DATE / TIME

NOTES

Made in the USA
Las Vegas, NV
17 November 2024

12012742R10057